ice creams & sorbets

COOL RECIPES

By Lou Seibert Pappas

Photographs by Victoria Pearson

CHRONICLE BOOKS
SAN FRANCISCO

Library of Congress Cataloging-in-Publication Data:
Pappas, Lou Seibert.
   Ice creams & sorbets : cool recipes / by Lou Seibert
Pappas ;
Photographs by Victoria Pearson.
      p. cm.
Includes index.
ISBN-10: 0-8118-4603-2 ISBN-13: 978-0-8118-4603-5
1. Ice cream, ices, etc. I. Title: Ice creams & sorbets. II.
Title.
TX795.P24 2005
641.8'62—dc22
                       2004007357

Manufactured in China.
Design and typesetting by Carole Goodman,
   Blue Anchor Design
Food stylist: Camille Renk
Prop stylist: Yolande Yorke–Edgell
Photographer's assistant: Jon Nakano
Food stylist's assistant: Jose Ortiz
Prop stylist's assistant: Nori Hubbs

Distributed in Canada by Raincoast Books
9050 Shaughnessy Street
Vancouver, British Columbia V6P 6E5

10 9 8 7 6 5 4 3 2

Chronicle Books LLC
680 Second Street
San Francisco, California 94107

www.chroniclebooks.com

Amaretto® is a registered trademark of Monterey
Mushrooms, Inc., Baci® is a registered trademark of
Société des Produits Nestlé S.A., Campari® is a regis-
tered trademark of Davide Campari Milano S.P.A.,
Cointreau® is a registered trademark of Cointreau
Corporation, Cuisinart® is a registered trademark of
Conair Corporation, De'Longhi® is a registered trade-
mark of De'Longhi S.P.A., Frangelico® is a registered
trademark of Giorgio Barbero & Figli S.P.A., Grand
Marnier® is a registered trademark of Société des
Produits Marnier-Lapostolle, KitchenAid® is a registered
trademark of Whirlpool Properties, Inc., Meyer® is a
registered trademark of Meyer Tomatoes, LLC, Nutella®
is a registered trademark of Ferrero S.P.A., Strega® is
a registered trademark of S.P.A. Strega Alberti
Benevento (S.A.B.).

My advice to you is not to inquire
why or whither, but just enjoy your ice
cream while it's on your plate. . . .

—Thornton Niven Wilder

TABLE OF CONTENTS

INTRODUCTION

It's fascinating to consider the changes in ice cream over the years. My passion for this luscious, cool, sweet crystallized in childhood—I got to lick the dasher of the homemade vanilla bean, peppermint, chocolate, and fresh strawberry ice creams. Later with home refrigerator-freezers, we indulged in packaged ice creams, as churning the homemade version seemed old-fashioned and a bother working with ice and salt. Then many trips to Europe, sampling sorbets, gelati, and ices in Italy, France, and Scandinavia, reignited my love for making my own. Plus the new, small, electric ice cream freezers made it a breeze!

When I wrote a previous book in the nineties, the recipe collection drew on my best samples of trips abroad and in America. The recipes featured the pistachio, framboise, and café flavors from Berthillon, the Parisian shop that schoolchildren adore. They covered stellar citrus and berry sorbets from three-star Michelin restaurants and fresh fruit ices from Turkey, South Africa, and Malaysia. Gelati were Grand Marnier and rum raisin versions from Florence, and the treat from Tivoli in Scandinavia was ultracreamy almond praline.

Today, frozen desserts are in the spotlight, with endless complexity in their flavors and presentations and the great delight they offer.

Yet what is really fun is to create your own. You can achieve silky, satiny ice cream unadorned with additives. You can turn out healthful, pure fruit ices and sorbets flaunting the fresh peak-of-season taste.

We are blessed with a wealth of products not widely available a short time ago. Lavender, basil, lemongrass, ginger, rosemary, blood orange, papaya, and exotic melons enhance this collection. Honey, red wine, and liqueurs lend an intriguing flavor and an appealing spoonable consistency to the products. In the toppings, balsamic vinegar uplifts berries and caramelized spiced nuts provide a teasing sugary crunch.

There is such a joy in turning seasonal bounty into an almost instant treat. The mix goes together readily in advance for chilling. With today's efficient equipment, ice cream can be churned in a quarter of an hour or so. Sorbets and ices can be easily frozen without a machine. So indulge. One luscious taste calls for another.

—*Lou Seibert Pappas*

THEORY AND TECHNIQUES

Ice cream is basically a liquid mixture that is stabilized by freezing much of the liquid and creating a very fine crystalline structure. The proportion of the ingredients and the preparation technique determine the quality. To achieve a fine consistency, several factors are important. Proper agitation is one. Others are rapid freezing and the amount of air incorporated.

It is useful to understand the science behind the freezing process. Harold McGee, in his book *On Food and Cooking,* explains that sugar lowers the freezing point of the solution from 32°F to around 27°F. The dissolved sugar gets in the way of the water molecules that would bond together to form ice crystals. At this temperature the water molecules have slowed enough so that their attraction becomes stronger than the disruptive influence of the sugar. As they crystallize, water molecules are subtracted from the mixture, the remaining solution gets more concentrated with sugar, and the freezing point is lowered further. Even when ice cream is frozen it will still contain some liquid at 0°F. The desirable temperature for serving is 10°F, as the proportion of liquid will then yield a semisolid consistency.

Therefore, to achieve a fine-quality product, ice creams, sorbets, and ices must have many well-dispersed tiny ice crystals. Otherwise, a few large crystals would yield an icy, coarse product. Though ice creams, sorbets, ices, and still-frozen desserts are considered to be "frozen," they are not completely so. Instead, tiny ice crystals are suspended in a binding syrup of sugar, with or without fat and/or protein. While much of the water in the mixture freezes, the concentration of sugar and other substances prevents the dessert from fully solidifying. Cream, milk, and eggs work as buffers to separate tiny crystals from one another. Alternatively, liquor, liqueurs, wine, honey, and corn syrup lower the freezing point of the mixture, so frozen desserts made with them will usually be softer. These additions are advantageous in homemade ice cream and sorbets, which sometimes get harder than commercial ice creams that have added emulsifiers.

Another influence on the ultimate texture is the amount of air whipped in. When the mixture churns in an ice cream maker, air beaten in helps keep the crystals apart and makes the texture smooth. Once the ice cream begins to thicken and becomes viscous, it starts to retain air well. As home freezers churn, the majority of the aeration happens toward the end of the processing time, producing tiny air pockets.

With ice cream, rapid cooling of the custard during stirring develops many small "seed" ice crystals and helps to distribute them evenly. If the mixture is also stirred while freezing, the ice masses are interfered with and the remaining ice will be in the form of tiny crystals. Ultimately, the more agitation provided, the slower the freezing process, and the tinier the ice crystals.

Granite are an exception to the goal of agitation, as large ice crystals are desired and so stirring is of short duration.

Three stages are involved in the preparation of frozen desserts. They include preparing the mix, freezing it, and ripening or firming it after the freezing process.

FREEZING ICE CREAM

After being frozen in an ice cream maker, ice cream is usually placed in the freezer for 2 hours to firm up, or "ripen." This allows the flavors to blend. Ideally, ice cream should be stored at fairly low temperatures, between -10° and 0°F, to maintain its fine texture and flavor. Cover it tightly so it doesn't pick up off odors and so that moisture does not settle onto its surface, forming large crystals. A sheet of plastic wrap pressed onto the surface of the ice cream is a good idea. The gradual coarsening of texture during freezing is due to repeated partial thawing when serving or from fluctuations in the temperature of the freezer.

Ice crystals grow during storage because whenever ice cream is warmed slightly, the smallest crystals melt. When the temperature drops again, the additional water is taken up by the surviving crystals, which get larger and larger. The effect is commonly known as "freezer burn." The lower the average storage temperature of the freezer, the less change takes place.

SERVING TIPS

Sorbets, ice creams, ices, and frozen yogurts should be allowed to warm to about 10°F before serving for the best flavor and texture. This allows them to achieve a slightly creamy consistency rather than a solid one. If ice cream is firmly frozen, transfer it to the refrigerator for 20 to 30 minutes before scooping and serving, but don't let it thaw too much as repeated thawing and refreezing will degrade its texture. Frozen products with honey, corn syrup, liqueur, or other alcohol as an ingredient will initially freeze to a softer consistency and may be spoonable directly from the freezer.

It is helpful to dip your ice cream scoop in a bowl of hot water before each scoop to make neat balls when scooping many servings of ice cream or sorbet.

Granite should be served slightly thawed and slushy. They are best served the day they are made, since the ice crystals will get larger as granite are stored.

GLOSSARY

Gelato (plural *gelati*): Italian ice cream, characterized by intense flavor and often served semifrozen. In Italy, each café often makes its own gelati with fresh fruits and other pure ingredients. The word *gelato* refers to various styles of ice cream, from light to rich versions.

Glace: The French word for ice cream

Granita (plural *granite;* French: *granité*): A type of Italian ice that is coarse in texture and often less intensely flavored than sorbetto. Minimal stirring during freezing characterizes the preparation of granite.

Ice: A coarsely textured frozen mixture of water, sugar, and liquid flavoring such as fruit juice, wine, coffee, or tea. Ices in this book are a cross between sorbets and granite.

Ice cream: A frozen confection made from milk and/or cream, sugar or another sweetener, and a flavoring such as chocolate, nuts, fruit, or spices. By FDA standards, packaged ice cream must contain a minimum of 10 percent butter-fat (8 percent for some flavors), 16 to 20 percent milk solids, and not more than 50 percent overrun. Premium ice creams and French-style ice creams usually have a cooked egg custard base.

Semifreddo: An Italian ice cream lightened with whipped cream, custard, or beaten egg yolks or whites and often a sugar syrup. The word means "half-frozen."

Sorbet: The French word for a frozen mixture that is finer in texture and usually more intensely flavored than an ice. Sorbets are usually made from fruit purées, water, and sugar.

Sorbetto (plural *sorbetti*): Italian sorbet

Plan to serve homemade ices, sorbets, and frozen yogurts within 1 to 2 days from the time they are made. Then they are at their best consistency. With longer storage, the smooth texture develops larger ice crystals. However, ice cream made with a cooked egg custard will keep longer, for several days or up to a week.

TYPES OF FROZEN DESSERTS

Sorbet and ice

Sorbet is basically fruit purée enhanced with sugar syrup, while ice is typically made of flavored liquid and sugar. They both work very well when frozen in a pan just until solid and then whipped to a frothy state in an electric mixer or food processor fitted with the metal blade. Be careful to not let the mixture thaw thoroughly in the process of whipping in the air.

Granita

The Italian word *granita* refers to the rough, grainy texture of this frozen dessert. Often it has minimal sugar. No machine is required to prepare this coarsely textured ice, since its uneven texture is best achieved by simply freezing in a pan and stirring several times with a fork to separate the largest ice crystals.

Ice cream

Custard that includes egg yolks is often the basis for ice cream. It is important to prepare an ice bath in a bowl or large pan to have ready before starting to cook the custard. Cook the mixture in the top of the double boiler over steaming water just until the custard coats the back of a spoon in an opaque layer, about 10 minutes. Once it has been cooked, it should be cooled immediately in the ice bath, to prevent curdling. Then refrigerate it to cool to 40°F. Once cream is added, stirring before freezing should be minimal as the fat particles could turn to flecks of butter. Add any liqueur during the last minute of churning as it retards freezing and softens the consistency. Sauces that are meant to swirl should be cooled thoroughly and blended in at the end of churning. Additives such as nuts should be room temperature or cooler and should be incorporated in the last 15 seconds.

Gelato

This Italian-style ice cream is characterized by intense flavor and a denser consistency than traditional ice cream because it contains less air. It is often served semifrozen. Gelato is made in an ice cream maker in the same fashion as ice cream.

Semifreddo

Semifreddo is Italian for "partially frozen." Sugar syrup beaten into egg yolks creates the especially airy, mousselike texture of this frozen dessert.

INGREDIENTS

Many commercial ice cream manufacturers use emulsifiers and stabilizers to improve the texture of their ice cream. This is not necessary in homemade ice cream prepared in small quantities with top-quality ingredients. Following is a summary of the ways in which many ice cream ingredients work to create a particular texture or flavor.

Note: These recipes were tested with whole milk, large eggs, and unsalted butter.

Note: A medium bowl works well for combining ingredients, unless otherwise specified.

Cream

The butterfat in heavy (whipping) cream is responsible for the rich, smooth texture of ice cream. Using all cream, however, increases the chance of producing ice cream flecked with butter, and too much fat can give the dessert a sticky, heavy texture. Using some milk or half-and-half lightens the texture.

Eggs

Egg yolks act as emulsifiers in a custard base and keep the fat globules in the cream from clumping together. They also create a rich texture and add an attractive yellow color to lighter colored ice creams. Because of current cholesterol concerns, the number of egg yolks used here is scaled back slightly from classic recipes of previous years.

Fruit

Most fruits contain pectin and fiber, which help keep milk fat and water molecules in an even suspension.

Half-and-half or milk

Milk fat forms small globules and helps keep the water molecules dispersed.

Sugar

Water in which sugar (or honey or corn syrup) has dissolved has a freezing point below 32°F. Because of the sugar, not all the water in the mixture freezes and the ice cream does not become completely solid.

Lavender, rosemary, and ginger

These herbs are steeped in liquid or sugar syrup to infuse their flavor, strained, and the liquid added to the dessert base.

Nuts, candies, wine, and liqueurs

These ingredients add flavor and sometimes texture. In churned desserts, nuts and candies are best added when the mixture is almost frozen, and any alcoholic ingredients should be added at the end of the freezing cycle because they retard the freezing process. (See page 13 for ideas.)

ICE CREAM MAKERS

Manufacturers offer ice cream makers to suit every budget. If the ice cream maker is the type packed with ice and salt, rock salt is preferred to table salt for several reasons. It is cheaper, it is less likely to sift through the ice and fall to the bottom, and it dissolves more slowly, lowering the temperature more gradually. A brine that is too cold will produce a coarse ice cream with too little incorporated air. A good proportion of ice to rock salt is 8 parts ice to 1 part salt, by measure.

Ice cream should be made according to the manufacturer's instructions for the ice cream maker. When filling an ice cream maker with ice cream mixture, allow an ample head space of 2 to 3 inches, as the mixture will expand during freezing when air is whipped in. This aeration, called "overrun" or "loft," improves the texture of the ice cream and prevents it from becoming a solid block of ice. Commercial freezers can pump in compressed air at the end of the freezing cycle, resulting in up to a 50 to 100 percent overrun. They also freeze at very low temperatures in minutes. Home freezers generally have only a 25 percent overrun.

One of the best freezers for the price is the Cuisinart ice cream maker, an electric machine with a cylindrical container that must be prefrozen. A compact (and stylish) design, it produces up to $1\frac{1}{2}$ quarts of excellent, smooth ice cream in 15 to 20 minutes. A transparent lid with an ingredient spout makes it easy to add ingredients at the end of the cycle.

QUICK ICE CREAM FLAVORS

Almond Toffee Ice Cream: Finely chop 4 ounces almond toffee or Almond Roca candy. Soften 1 quart vanilla ice cream, sprinkle the candy pieces over, and fold in. Freeze 2 hours, or until firm.

Biscotti Cookie Bar Ice Cream: Finely chop two 2-ounce chocolate-almond biscotti. Soften 1 quart vanilla or coffee ice cream, sprinkle the biscotti pieces over, and fold in. Freeze 2 hours, or until firm.

Brownie Ice Cream: Crumble enough brownies to make $1\frac{1}{4}$ cups large crumbs. Soften 1 quart vanilla, coffee, or chocolate ice cream, sprinkle the brownie pieces over, and fold in. Freeze 2 hours, or until firm.

Candied Chestnut Ice Cream: Drain one 8-ounce jar whole chestnuts in syrup, reserving the syrup. Chop the chestnuts into pieces the size of hazelnuts. Fold them into 1 quart softened vanilla or eggnog ice cream. Freeze 2 hours, or until firm. Heat the syrup with 2 tablespoons cognac and serve scoops of ice cream with the warm syrup.

Candied Orange Peel Ice Cream: Chop candied orange peel to make $\frac{2}{3}$ cup. Soften 1 quart coffee or chocolate ice cream, sprinkle the orange peel over, and fold in. Freeze 2 hours, or until firm.

Chocolate Cherry Ice Cream: Soften 1 quart vanilla or chocolate ice cream and fold in 2 tablespoons kirsch and $\frac{2}{3}$ cup chocolate-covered dried cherries. Freeze 2 hours, or until firm.

Peppermint Candy Ice Cream: Finely chop 4 ounces peppermint candies or candy canes.

Soften 1 quart vanilla ice cream, sprinkle the candy pieces over, and fold in. Freeze 2 hours, or until firm.

The De'Longhi ice cream maker from Italy is an expensive compact compressor machine with a built-in freezer. It features a double paddle that mixes thoroughly and prepares frozen desserts in 20 to 40 minutes. The anodized aluminum bowl removes for serving and hand washing.

The Rolls Royce of ice cream makers is the stainless steel KitchenAid Pro Line Frozen Dessert Maker, an ultraexpensive electric machine with self-contained refrigeration that produces up to 2 quarts of ice cream in about 30 minutes. A built-in funnel and pusher simplify adding main ingredients as well as mix-ins.

The traditional White Mountain hand-cranked wooden ice cream bucket is still on the market, as it has been for over a century. It is also available in an electric version. Both kinds come in a range of sizes.

In addition to the currently available ice cream makers, many home kitchens have older machines in the pantry. The Donvier manual model and its clones use a cylinder container that must be frozen ahead. It requires hand cranking every few minutes during churning.

The Vitantonio Gelato model is a manual maker with a cylinder container that must be frozen ahead and hand cranked every 4 or 5 minutes during the freezing time. An electric model is available by the same brand.

The Simac II Gelataio Magnum is a high-end electric machine with a self-contained refrigeration system. The unit is more difficult to wash than most models.

The Rival electric ice cream maker has a metal canister and a lightweight wooden bucket that uses ice and salt like old-fashioned makers.

EQUIPMENT

- Double boiler, preferably 2-quart size but 3 quart size works well

- Electric ice cream freezer (see page 12)

- One-quart plastic container for refrigerating the ice cream: Plastic works well because if you are in a hurry, you can put it in the freezer briefly to chill. This container is also perfect for freezing the ice cream when churned. Optionally, smaller 1 pint or ½ pint containers are useful if you are serving just two persons.

- Rasp-style grater for zesting citrus

- Silicone spatula that handles heat up to 500°F: A silicone spatula is ideal for stirring the custard as it cleans the sides of the pan neatly. Or, you can use a metal or black-coated spoon, depending on the surface of your double boiler.

ICE
CREAMS

THIS TANTALIZING COLLECTION ENCOMPASSES A WEALTH

of flavors, from old-fashioned classics such as vanilla bean, strawberry, and bittersweet chocolate, to contemporary delights incorporating ingredients like lavender, black currant tea, almond fudge, and liqueurs such as Strega.

Classic Vanilla Bean Ice Cream

This is one of the most versatile ice cream flavors—ideal as a topping on chocolate soufflé cake, fruit pies, and cobblers. Or mingle tiny scoopfuls in a tall glass with bittersweet chocolate and coffee ice creams or fruit sorbet. Flecks of vanilla bean imbue this creamy ice cream with an exotic flavor that surpasses vanilla extract alone.

One 4-inch vanilla bean

2 cups half-and-half or milk

4 large egg yolks

⅔ cup sugar

1 cup heavy (whipping) cream

Prepare a large bowl or pan of ice water.

Split the vanilla bean in half lengthwise and scrape the black seeds into the top of a double boiler. Add the vanilla bean and half-and-half, and heat over simmering water until steaming. In a bowl, whisk the egg yolks until blended, then whisk in the sugar. Whisk in about half of the hot half-and-half and pour the yolk mixture into the pan of half-and-half. Stir and cook over simmering water until the custard coats the back of a silicone spatula or spoon, about 10 minutes. Immediately place the custard pan in the ice bath and stir the custard occasionally until it cools to room temperature. Transfer to a container and stir in the cream. Cover and refrigerate until thoroughly chilled, about 3 hours.

When you are ready to freeze the mixture, remove the vanilla bean with a fork. Freeze the mixture in an ice cream maker according to the manufacturer's instructions. Transfer to a container, cover, and freeze until firm, about 2 hours.

MAKES ABOUT 1 QUART

Note: You may substitute 2 teaspoons vanilla extract for the vanilla bean. Stir it into the custard with the cream.

Mexican Chocolate–Cinnamon Swirl Ice Cream

A cinnamon candy swirl weaves a web throughout this creamy chocolate ice cream, tantalizing the palate with its spicy heat.

2 cups half-and-half or milk

2 cinnamon sticks or 1½ teaspoons ground cinnamon

3 large egg yolks

⅔ cup sugar

1 teaspoon instant espresso powder

4 ounces bittersweet chocolate, chopped

1 ounce unsweetened chocolate, chopped

1 cup heavy (whipping) cream

CINNAMON SWIRL
¼ cup packed dark brown sugar

¼ cup light corn syrup

2 teaspoons ground cinnamon

¼ cup half-and-half

1 tablespoon unsalted butter

Prepare a large bowl or pan of ice water.

In the top of a double boiler, heat the half-and-half and cinnamon over simmering water until steaming. Remove from the heat and steep for 15 minutes if using sticks, 5 minutes if using ground cinnamon. In a bowl, whisk the egg yolks until blended, then whisk in the ⅔ cup sugar and espresso powder. Whisk in about half of the hot half-and-half and pour the yolk mixture into the pan of half-and-half. Cook and stir over simmering water until the custard coats the back of a silicone spatula or spoon, about 10 minutes. Stir in the chocolates until they melt. Immediately place the custard pan in the ice bath and stir the custard occasionally until it cools to room temperature. Strain the custard into a container and discard the cinnamon sticks. Stir in the cream, cover, and refrigerate until thoroughly chilled, about 3 hours.

To make the Cinnamon Swirl: In a small saucepan, combine the sugar, corn syrup, and cinnamon. Bring to a boil and boil 2 minutes. Remove from the heat and stir in the half-and-half and butter. Pour into a container and let cool.

Freeze the custard in an ice cream maker according to the manufacturer's instructions. When the ice cream is almost frozen, pour in the Cinnamon Swirl and churn until blended in, about 15 seconds more. Transfer to a container, cover, and freeze until firm, about 2 hours.

MAKES ABOUT 1 QUART

Mocha–Hazelnut Crunch Ice Cream

Toasted buttery hazelnuts are marvelously crunchy in both the ice cream base and the caramelized praline that gilds the scoopfuls of this mocha ice cream. Try substituting almonds, walnuts, or pecans and using complementary liqueurs.

¾ cup (4 ounces) hazelnuts

2 cups half-and-half or milk

4 large egg yolks

⅔ cup plus 2 teaspoons sugar, divided

¼ cup unsweetened cocoa

1 teaspoon instant espresso powder

4 ounces bittersweet chocolate, chopped

1 ounce unsweetened chocolate, chopped

1 cup heavy (whipping) cream

½ teaspoon vanilla extract

1 teaspoon unsalted butter, plus extra for greasing

1 tablespoon Frangelico or other liqueur (optional)

Prepare a large bowl or pan of ice water.

Preheat the oven to 350°F. Place the nuts on a baking sheet with sides and bake until lightly toasted, about 8 to 10 minutes. Turn out the nuts onto a tea towel and rub together to remove their papery skins. Let cool. In a food processor or blender, blend ½ cup of the nuts until very finely ground and they start to release their oil. Chop the remaining nuts and set aside. Place the ground nuts in the top of a double boiler with the half-and-half and heat over simmering water until steaming. Remove from the heat and steep for 15 minutes.

In a bowl, whisk the egg yolks until blended, then whisk in the ⅔ cup sugar, cocoa, and espresso powder. Whisk in about half of the hot half-and-half and pour the yolk mixture into the pan of half-and-half. Stir and cook over simmering water until the custard coats the back of a silicone spatula or spoon, about 10 minutes. Stir in the chocolates until they melt. Immediately place the custard pan in the ice bath and stir the custard occasionally until it cools to room temperature. Transfer to a container and stir in the cream and vanilla. Cover and refrigerate until thoroughly chilled, about 3 hours.

Meanwhile, in a small skillet, melt the butter and add the reserved chopped nuts. Sprinkle with the remaining 2 teaspoons sugar and cook over medium heat, stirring until the nuts are caramelized, about 2 minutes. Remove to a buttered sheet of aluminum foil and let cool. When cool, grind the praline in a food processor or blender until chunky. Store in an airtight container until needed.

Freeze the custard in an ice cream maker according to the manufacturer's instructions. When the ice cream is almost frozen, spoon in the liqueur, if desired, and churn until blended in, about 1 minute more. Add in the hazelnut praline and churn until blended in, about 15 seconds more, or reserve it to sprinkle on top of the ice cream. Transfer to a container, cover, and freeze until firm, about 2 hours.

MAKES ABOUT 1 QUART

Mint Chocolate Chip Ice Cream

Use a high-quality bar of bittersweet chocolate to embellish this old-fashioned favorite. I like to use a chef's knife for shredding the chocolate bar into neat morsels, but you could also grate it on the large holes of a box grater. Or, chop the chocolate to make larger chunks in the ice cream.

2 cups half-and-half or milk

4 large egg yolks

½ cup sugar

1 cup heavy (whipping) cream

2 teaspoons peppermint extract

3 ounces bittersweet chocolate, shredded (about ⅔ cup)

Prepare a large bowl or pan of ice water.

In the top of a double boiler, heat the half-and-half over simmering water until steaming. In a bowl, whisk the egg yolks until blended, then whisk in the sugar. Whisk in about half of the hot half-and-half and pour the yolk mixture into the pan of half-and-half. Stir and cook over simmering water until the custard coats the back of a silicone spatula or spoon, about 10 minutes. Immediately place the custard pan in the ice bath and stir the custard occasionally until it cools to room temperature. Transfer to a container and stir in the cream and extract. Cover and refrigerate until thoroughly chilled, about 3 hours.

Freeze in an ice cream maker according to the manufacturer's instructions. When the ice cream is almost frozen, add the chocolate and churn until blended in, about 15 seconds more. Transfer to a container, cover, and freeze until firm, about 2 hours.

MAKES ABOUT 1 QUART

Chocolate Kiss Ice Cream

In Italy the chocolate hazelnut candy called *Baci* (which means "kiss" in Italian) makes addictive bitefuls. It is easy to replicate the flavor using the hazelnut spread Nutella as a shortcut. This makes an intensely dense ice cream, putting one in mind of chilled chocolate fudge.

2 cups half-and-half or milk

4 large egg yolks

½ cup plus 2 teaspoons sugar, divided

¼ cup unsweetened cocoa

1 tablespoon instant espresso powder

4 ounces bittersweet chocolate, chopped

1 cup heavy (whipping) cream

½ cup Nutella or other chocolate-hazelnut spread

⅓ cup (1½ ounces) hazelnuts

1 teaspoon unsalted butter plus extra for greasing

1 tablespoon Frangelico or Amaretto (optional)

Prepare a large bowl or pan of ice water.

In the top of a double boiler, heat the half-and-half over simmering water until steaming. In a bowl, whisk the egg yolks until blended, then whisk in the ½ cup sugar, cocoa, and espresso powder. Whisk in about half of the hot half-and-half and pour the yolk mixture into the pan of half-and-half. Stir and cook over simmering water until the custard coats the back of a silicone spatula or spoon, about 10 minutes. Stir in the chocolate until it melts. Immediately place the custard pan in the ice bath and stir the custard occasionally until it cools to room temperature. Transfer to a container and stir in the cream and Nutella. Cover and refrigerate until thoroughly chilled, about 3 hours.

Preheat the oven to 350°F. Place the nuts on a baking sheet with sides and bake until lightly toasted, about 8 to10 minutes. Turn out the nuts onto a tea towel and rub together to remove their papery skins. Let cool and finely chop.

In a small skillet, melt the butter and add the chopped nuts. Sprinkle with the remaining 2 teaspoons sugar and cook over medium heat, stirring until the nuts are caramelized, about 2 minutes. Remove to a buttered sheet of aluminum foil and let cool. When cool, grind the praline in a food processor or blender until chunky. Store in an airtight container until needed.

Freeze the custard in an ice cream maker according to the manufacturer's instructions. When the ice cream is almost frozen, spoon in the liqueur, if desired, and churn until blended in, about 1 minute more. Add the hazelnut praline and churn until blended in, about 15 seconds more. Transfer to a container, cover, and freeze until firm, about 2 hours.

MAKES ABOUT 1 QUART

Bittersweet Chocolate Ice Cream

A top-quality bittersweet chocolate lends an intense flavor to this ice cream. You can experiment with several brands and enjoy the subtle differences.

2 cups half-and-half or milk

3 large egg yolks

$\frac{2}{3}$ cup sugar

6 ounces bittersweet chocolate, chopped

1 ounce unsweetened chocolate, chopped

1 cup heavy (whipping) cream

1 teaspoon vanilla extract

Prepare a large bowl or pan of ice water.

In the top of a double boiler, heat the half-and-half over simmering water until steaming. In a bowl, whisk the egg yolks until blended, then whisk in the sugar. Whisk in about half of the hot half-and-half and pour the yolk mixture into the pan of half-and-half. Stir and cook over simmering water until the custard coats the back of a silicone spatula or spoon, about 10 minutes. Stir in the chocolates until they melt. Immediately place the custard pan in the ice bath and stir the custard occasionally until it cools to room temperature. Transfer to a container and stir in the cream and vanilla. Cover and refrigerate until thoroughly chilled, about 3 hours.

Freeze in an ice cream maker according to the manufacturer's instructions. Transfer to a container, cover, and freeze until firm, about 2 hours.

MAKES ABOUT 1 QUART

Mocha Almond Fudge Ice Cream

Try this coffee-flavored ice cream with biscotti on the side, just as you would with the mocha almond cappuccino that inspired this treat.

⅔ cup (3 ounces) chopped almonds

2 cups half-and-half or milk

6 tablespoons coffee beans or
  3 tablespoons instant coffee powder

4 large egg yolks

⅔ cup sugar

1 cup heavy (whipping) cream

CHOCOLATE FUDGE

2 tablespoons sugar

2 tablespoons unsweetened cocoa

¼ cup light corn syrup

2 tablespoons half-and-half

1 tablespoon unsalted butter

¼ teaspoon vanilla extract

Prepare a large bowl or pan of ice water.

Preheat the oven to 350°F. Place the nuts on a baking sheet with sides and bake until lightly toasted, about 8 to 10 minutes. Set aside to cool.

In the top of a double boiler, heat the half-and-half and coffee beans over simmering water until steaming. Remove from the heat and steep for 40 minutes, or until the coffee flavor is pronounced to your liking. (If using the coffee powder, mix it into the hot half-and-half until dissolved.)

In a bowl, whisk the egg yolks until blended, then whisk in the sugar. Whisk in about half of the hot half-and-half and pour the yolk mixture into the pan of half-and-half. Stir and cook over simmering water until the custard coats the back of a silicone spatula or spoon, about 10 minutes. Immediately place the custard pan in the ice bath and stir the custard occasionally until it cools to room temperature. Strain the custard into a container and discard the beans. Stir in the cream, cover, and refrigerate until thoroughly chilled, about 3 hours.

Meanwhile, prepare the Chocolate Fudge: In a small saucepan, combine the sugar and cocoa. Stir in the corn syrup and half-and-half. Stirring constantly, heat over medium heat until the mixture comes to a boil. Reduce heat. Simmer 2 minutes and stir in the butter and vanilla. Let cool to room temperature.

Freeze the custard in an ice cream maker according to the manufacturer's instructions. When the ice cream is almost frozen, spoon in the Chocolate Fudge and the toasted almonds and churn until blended in, about 15 seconds more. Transfer to a container, cover, and freeze until firm, about 2 hours.

MAKES ABOUT 1 QUART

Kona Coffee Ice Cream

Whole coffee beans lend a seductive richness to this ice cream. Choose a bean with an aroma you like, such as a Kona or Mocha Java. As a shortcut, you can substitute 3 tablespoons instant coffee powder for the beans and eliminate the steeping time. Sticky Hot Fudge Sauce (page 92) and Butterscotch Caramel Sauce (page 89) are wonderful toppings on goblets of this ice cream.

2 cups half-and-half or milk

6 tablespoons coffee beans or
  3 tablespoons instant coffee powder

4 large egg yolks

⅔ cup sugar

1 cup heavy (whipping) cream

Prepare a large bowl or pan of ice water.

In the top of a double boiler, heat the half-and-half and coffee beans over simmering water until steaming. Remove from the heat and steep for 40 minutes, or until the coffee flavor is pronounced to your liking. (If using the coffee powder, mix it into the hot half-and-half until dissolved.)

In a bowl, whisk the egg yolks until blended, then whisk in the sugar. Whisk in about half of the hot half-and-half and pour the yolk mixture into the pan of half-and-half. Stir and cook over simmering water until the custard coats the back of a silicone spatula or spoon, about 10 minutes. Immediately place the custard pan in the ice bath and stir the custard occasionally until it cools to room temperature. Strain the custard into a container and discard the beans. Stir in the cream, cover, and refrigerate until thoroughly chilled, about 3 hours.

Freeze in an ice cream maker according to the manufacturer's instructions. Transfer to a container, cover, and freeze until firm, about 2 hours.

MAKES ABOUT 1 QUART

Hazelnut Ice Cream

Called *nocciola* in Italy and *noisette* in France, hazelnut gelato, glace, or ice cream is a beloved flavor of mine. I love to pair it with small scoopfuls of other flavors, such as bittersweet chocolate and raspberry. The nuts should be finely ground to release their oils.

⅔ cup (3 ounces) hazelnuts

2 cups half-and-half or milk

4 large egg yolks

⅔ cup sugar

1 cup heavy (whipping) cream

1 teaspoon vanilla extract

Prepare a large bowl or pan of ice water.

Preheat the oven to 350°F. Place the nuts on a baking sheet with sides and bake until lightly toasted, about 8 to10 minutes. Turn out the nuts onto a tea towel and rub together to remove their papery skins. Let cool. In a food processor or blender, blend the nuts until finely ground.

In the top of a double boiler, heat the half-and-half and nuts over simmering water until steaming. Remove from the heat and steep for 15 minutes.

In a bowl, whisk the egg yolks until blended, then whisk in the sugar. Whisk in about half of the hot half-and-half and pour the yolk mixture into the pan of half-and-half. Stir and cook over simmering water until the custard coats the back of a silicone spatula or spoon, about 10 minutes. Immediately place the custard pan in the ice bath and stir the custard occasionally until it cools to room temperature. Transfer to a container and stir in the cream and vanilla. Cover and refrigerate until thoroughly chilled, about 3 hours.

Freeze in an ice cream maker according to the manufacturer's instructions. Transfer to a container, cover, and freeze until firm, about 2 hours.

MAKES ABOUT 1 QUART

Variations:
Hazelnut Chocolate Flake Ice Cream: Prepare Hazelnut Ice Cream as directed above. When the ice cream is almost frozen, add ⅓ cup (2 ounces) shredded bittersweet chocolate and churn until blended in, about 15 seconds more.

Toasted Almond Ice Cream: Substitute 3 ounces natural (skin on) almonds for the hazelnuts. When the ice cream is almost frozen, spoon in 2 tablespoons Amaretto and churn until blended in, about 1 minute more.

Pralines and Cream Ice Cream

Caramelized pecans lace this ice cream with a candy crunch for a versatile flavor that is wonderful with fruit desserts, warm chocolate cake, or gingerbread. Pecan pralines are a classic candy in Louisiana, where they are eaten as crunchy or chewy patties.

2 cups half-and-half or milk

4 large egg yolks

⅔ cup packed dark brown sugar

1 cup heavy (whipping) cream

1 teaspoon vanilla extract

PECAN PRALINE

1 tablespoon honey

1 tablespoon packed dark brown sugar

1 tablespoon water

½ teaspoon ground cardamom

1 cup (4 ounces) pecans

1 teaspoon unsalted butter, melted, plus extra for greasing

Prepare a large bowl or pan of ice water.

In the top of a double boiler, heat the half-and-half over simmering water until steaming. In a bowl, whisk the egg yolks until blended, then whisk in the sugar. Whisk in about half of the hot half-and-half and pour the yolk mixture into the pan of half-and-half. Stir and cook over simmering water until the custard coats the back of a silicone spatula or spoon, about 10 minutes. Immediately place the custard pan in the ice bath and stir the custard occasionally until it cools to room temperature. Transfer to a container and stir in the cream and vanilla. Cover and refrigerate until thoroughly chilled, about 3 hours.

To make the Pecan Praline: Preheat the oven to 350°F. Line a baking sheet with sides with aluminum foil and grease it lightly. In a small, heavy saucepan, heat the honey, sugar, water, and cardamom over medium heat until the mixture comes to a boil. Reduce heat, then simmer 2 minutes. Mix in the nuts and stir to coat thoroughly. Turn out onto the foil-lined pan. Bake until lightly toasted, about 8 to10 minutes. Remove from the foil and toss with the butter in a small bowl. Let cool. Store in an airtight container until needed.

Freeze the custard in an ice cream maker according to the manufacturer's instructions. When the ice cream is almost frozen, add ¾ of the praline and churn until blended in, about 15 seconds more. Transfer to a container, cover, and freeze until firm, about 2 hours. Sprinkle the remaining praline over the ice cream at serving time.

MAKES ABOUT 1 QUART

Variation:
Maple-Walnut Ice Cream: When making the custard, substitute ⅔ cup maple syrup for the brown sugar. For the caramelized nuts, substitute 1 tablespoon maple syrup for the brown sugar and walnuts for the pecans. Use ground cinnamon in place of the cardamom.

Honey-Orange-Pistachio Ice Cream

Sugared pistachios lend a savory crunch to this ambrosial honey- and orange-scented ice cream. A splash of orange liqueur softens the texture to create a creamy consistency for easy scooping directly from the freezer. Put a dollop over fresh sliced peaches or nectarines and enjoy with crisp biscotti.

1 tablespoon unsalted butter

⅔ cup (3 ounces) pistachios

2 tablespoons plus 1 teaspoon sugar, divided

2 tablespoons grated orange zest

2 cups half-and-half or milk

4 large egg yolks

⅔ cup honey

1 cup heavy (whipping) cream

2 tablespoons Cointreau, Grand Marnier, or other orange liqueur (optional)

Prepare a large bowl or pan of ice water.

In a small skillet, melt the butter over medium heat. Add the nuts, and sprinkle with the 2 tablespoons sugar. Cook, stirring continuously, until the nuts are toasted and caramelized, about 2 minutes. Set aside to cool.

In a small bowl, mash the zest with the remaining 1 teaspoon sugar to release the oils. In the top of a double boiler, heat the half-and-half over simmering water until steaming. In a bowl, whisk the egg yolks until blended, then whisk in the honey and sugared zest. Whisk in about half of the hot half-and-half and pour the yolk mixture into the pan of half-and-half. Stir and cook over simmering water until the custard coats the back of a silicone spatula or spoon, about 10 minutes. Immediately place the custard pan in the ice bath and stir the custard occasionally until it cools to room temperature. Transfer to a container and stir in the cream. Cover and refrigerate until thoroughly chilled, about 3 hours.

Freeze in an ice cream maker according to the manufacturer's instructions. When the ice cream is almost frozen, spoon in the liqueur, if desired, and churn until blended in, about 1 minute more. Add the nuts and churn until blended in, about 15 seconds more. Transfer to a container, cover, and freeze until firm, about 2 hours.

MAKES ABOUT 1 QUART

Crystallized Ginger Ice Cream

Hot, sweet bites of ginger surprise your palate in this creamy, smooth ice cream, which gets an additional lift from fresh ginger. Pair this frosty confection with a tropical fruit plate or partner it with Caramel Swirl–Macadamia Nut Ice Cream (page 38) or Bittersweet Chocolate Ice Cream (page 25) for a delicious duo.

2 cups half-and-half or milk

¼ cup minced peeled fresh ginger

4 large egg yolks

⅔ cup sugar

1 cup heavy (whipping) cream

1 teaspoon vanilla extract

⅓ cup chopped crystallized ginger

Prepare a large bowl or pan of ice water.

In the top of a double boiler, heat the half-and-half and fresh ginger over simmering water until steaming. Remove from the heat and steep for 15 minutes. In a bowl, whisk the egg yolks until blended, then whisk in the sugar. Whisk in about half of the hot half-and-half and pour the yolk mixture into the pan of half-and-half. Stir and cook over simmering water until the custard coats the back of a silicone spatula or spoon, about 10 minutes. Immediately place the custard pan in the ice bath and stir the custard occasionally until it cools to room temperature. Strain the custard into a container and discard the ginger. Stir in the cream and vanilla, cover, and refrigerate until thoroughly chilled, about 3 hours.

Freeze in an ice cream maker according to the manufacturer's instructions. When the ice cream is almost frozen, add the crystallized ginger and churn until blended in, about 15 seconds more. Transfer to a container, cover, and freeze until firm, about 2 hours.

MAKES ABOUT 1 QUART

Eggnog Ice Cream

Holiday eggnog creates an ultrarich and creamy ice cream with a lovely nutmeg overtone. It welcomes a splash of brandy or bourbon drizzled overtop. You couldn't go wrong topping warm pumpkin or pecan pie with scoops of this ice cream.

½ cup milk

½ cup sugar

2 cups eggnog

Freshly ground nutmeg to taste

¾ cup heavy (whipping) cream

2 tablespoons brandy or bourbon

Prepare a large bowl or pan of ice water.

Combine the milk and sugar in a medium saucepan and heat, stirring, to dissolve the sugar. Stir in the eggnog and nutmeg. Place the pan in the ice bath and stir occasionally until it cools to room temperature. Transfer to a container and stir in the cream. Cover and refrigerate until thoroughly chilled, about 3 hours.

Freeze in an ice cream maker according to the manufacturer's instructions. When the ice cream is almost frozen, spoon in the brandy and churn until blended in, about 1 minute more. Transfer to a container, cover, and freeze until firm, about 2 hours.

MAKES ABOUT 1 QUART

Dulce de Leche Ice Cream

Butterscotch chips imbue this classic Mexican flavor with rich caramel. The candy nuggets add a cool, crisp bite and, if you are a nut aficionado, roasted cashews are a delicious addition. Add 1 cup coarsely chopped roasted nuts during the last 15 seconds of churning.

2 cups half-and-half or milk

4 large egg yolks

½ cup sugar

2 cups (12 ounces) butterscotch chips, divided

1 cup heavy (whipping) cream

1 teaspoon vanilla extract

Prepare a large bowl or pan of ice water.

In the top of a double boiler, heat the half-and-half over simmering water until steaming. In a bowl, whisk the egg yolks until blended, then whisk in the sugar. Whisk in about half of the hot half-and-half and pour the yolk mixture into the pan of half-and-half. Stir with a silicone spatula or spoon and cook over simmering water for about 8 minutes. Stir in 1 cup of the chips and continue stirring until blended in and the custard coats the back of the spatula, about 2 minutes more. Immediately place the custard pan in the ice bath and stir the custard occasionally until it cools to room temperature. Transfer to a container and stir in the cream and vanilla. Cover and refrigerate until thoroughly chilled, about 3 hours.

Freeze in an ice cream maker according to the manufacturer's instructions. When the ice cream is almost frozen, add the remaining 1 cup chips and churn until blended in, about 15 seconds more. Transfer to a container, cover, and freeze until firm, about 2 hours.

MAKES ABOUT 1 QUART

Caramel Swirl–Macadamia Nut Ice Cream

Caramel laces this ice cream with chewy candy and the nuts lend crunch for a delicious topping on fresh sliced peaches or an open-face pear tart.

2 cups half-and-half or milk

4 large egg yolks

⅔ cup sugar

1 cup heavy (whipping) cream

2 teaspoons vanilla extract

CARAMEL SAUCE

½ cup sugar

¼ cup half-and-half

2 tablespoons plus 1 teaspoon unsalted butter, divided

1 tablespoon light corn syrup

½ cup (2½ ounces) macadamia nuts, Brazil nuts, or pecans, chopped

Prepare a large bowl or pan of ice water.

In the top of a double boiler, heat the half-and-half over simmering water until steaming. In a bowl, whisk the egg yolks until blended, then whisk in the sugar. Whisk in about half of the hot half-and-half and pour the yolk mixture into the pan of half-and-half. Stir and cook over simmering water until the custard coats the back of a silicone spatula or spoon, about 10 minutes. Immediately place the custard pan in the ice bath and stir the custard occasionally until it cools to room temperature. Transfer to a container and stir in the cream and vanilla. Cover and refrigerate until chilled, about 3 hours.

To make the Caramel Sauce: Heat the sugar in a small, heavy saucepan over medium heat, swirling the pan occasionally, until it caramelizes to a light amber color, 5 to 7 minutes. (If the sugar crystallizes on the sides of the pan before melting, put a lid on the pan to help wash down the sugar crystals.) Stir in the half-and-half, 2 tablespoons of the butter, and corn syrup. Cook and stir until smooth and slightly thickened, about 2 minutes. Let cool to room temperature.

In a small saucepan, toast the nuts in the remaining 1 teaspoon butter until golden; let cool to room temperature.

Freeze the custard in an ice cream maker according to the manufacturer's instructions. When the ice cream is almost frozen, add the caramel sauce and nuts and churn until blended in, about 15 seconds more. Transfer to a container, cover, and freeze until firm, about 2 hours.

MAKES ABOUT 1 QUART

Goat Cheese–Herb Ice Cream

This is a wonderful savory ice cream to turn out in 15 minutes or less. Fresh herbs add a fresh-from-the-garden flavor to accent chilled gazpacho or cucumber soup or to top fresh asparagus, grilled salmon, or trout. The churning time on this is very brief as it whips up more quickly due to its richness. Because you need only a small dollop for embellishment, it is smart to package the ice cream in small containers for each serving occasion.

1 cup buttermilk

6 ounces soft goat cheese

⅓ cup mixed minced fresh herbs: chives, parsley, tarragon, and marjoram

½ cup heavy (whipping) cream

In a food processor or blender, combine the buttermilk, cheese, and herbs. Process until the herbs are distributed. Add the cream and process just until blended in. Transfer to a container, cover, and refrigerate until thoroughly chilled, about 3 hours.

Freeze in an ice cream maker according to the manufacturer's instructions. (It will churn quickly—in about 7 minutes.) Serve immediately or transfer to small containers, cover, and freeze. To serve later, let stand in the refrigerator for 1 hour to soften slightly.

MAKES ABOUT 1½ PINTS

Strawberry Ice Cream

This luscious berry ice cream is one of the best of its kind. It is sublime alone or paired with Classic Vanilla Bean Ice Cream (page 17) or Grand Marnier Ice Cream (page 50). Top it with Sticky Hot Fudge Sauce (page 92) for a decadent treat or Blackberry-Balsamic Syrup (page 92) for a lighter dessert.

1 cup heavy (whipping) cream

½ cup half-and-half or milk

3 large egg yolks

¾ cup sugar, divided

2½ cups (about 1¼ pounds) fresh strawberries, hulled

1 tablespoon freshly squeezed lemon juice

Prepare a large bowl or pan of ice water.

In the top of a double boiler, heat the cream and half-and-half over simmering water until steaming. In a bowl, whisk the egg yolks until blended, then whisk in ½ cup of the sugar. Whisk in about half of the hot cream, and pour the yolk mixture into the pan of cream. Stir and cook over simmering water until the custard coats the back of a silicone spatula or spoon, about 10 minutes. Immediately place the custard pan in the ice bath and stir the custard occasionally until it cools to room temperature.

Meanwhile, in a bowl, mash the strawberries with a potato masher, sprinkle with the remaining ¼ cup sugar and the juice, and let stand until the sugar dissolves. Stir into the custard and transfer to a container. Cover and refrigerate until thoroughly chilled, about 3 hours.

Freeze in an ice cream maker according to the manufacturer's instructions. Transfer to a container, cover, and freeze until firm, about 2 hours.

MAKES ABOUT 1 QUART

Black Currant Tea Ice Cream

Tea leaves infuse this ice cream with an intriguing berry overtone. Garnish scoopfuls with a mingling of two or more fresh berries—raspberries, blackberries, blueberries, or strawberries—for a tantalizing pairing.

2 cups half-and-half or milk	⅔ cup sugar
¼ cup loose black currant tea leaves	1 cup heavy (whipping) cream
4 large egg yolks	

Prepare a large bowl or pan of ice water.

In the top of a double boiler, heat the half-and-half and tea, enclosed in a tea ball or cheesecloth, over simmering water until steaming. Remove from the heat and steep for 5 to 7 minutes for an intense flavor. Remove the tea ball. (If you do not have a tea ball, strain the tea through a fine-mesh sieve after steeping.) In a bowl, whisk the egg yolks until blended, then whisk in the sugar. Whisk in about half of the hot half-and-half and pour the yolk mixture into the pan of half-and-half. Stir and cook over simmering water until the custard coats the back of a silicone spatula or spoon, about 10 minutes. Immediately place the custard pan in the ice bath and stir the custard occasionally until it cools to room temperature. Transfer to a container and stir in the cream. Cover and refrigerate until thoroughly chilled, about 3 hours.

Freeze in an ice cream maker according to the manufacturer's instructions. Transfer to a container, cover, and freeze until firm, about 2 hours.

MAKES ABOUT 1 QUART

Variation:
Green Tea–Candied Orange Peel Ice Cream: Substitute ¼ cup green tea leaves for the black currant tea leaves. When the ice cream is almost frozen, add ½ cup chopped candied orange peel and churn until blended in, about 15 seconds more.

Peach Ice Cream

Full-flavored ripe peaches at the height of the season are a must for this ice cream. This is delicious with a shower of hazelnut praline (see page 20) or Butterscotch Caramel Sauce (page 89).

1 cup heavy (whipping) cream

½ cup half-and-half or milk

¾ cup sugar, divided

1¼ pounds ripe peaches
 (about 5 peaches)

2 tablespoons freshly squeezed
 lemon juice

1 teaspoon vanilla extract

¼ teaspoon almond extract

Freshly grated nutmeg (optional)

Prepare a large bowl or pan of ice water.

Combine the cream, half-and-half, and ½ cup of the sugar in a medium saucepan and heat over medium heat, stirring, to dissolve the sugar. Place the pan in the ice bath and stir occasionally until it cools to room temperature. Transfer to a container, cover, and refrigerate until thoroughly chilled, about 3 hours.

About an hour before you wish to freeze the ice cream, peel, pit, and slice the peaches. Sprinkle with the remaining ¼ cup sugar and the juice and mash in a bowl with a potato masher to crush the fruit or whirl in a food processor; let stand until the sugar dissolves. Stir into the cream mixture with the vanilla and almond, cover, and refrigerate for 1 hour. If desired, grate in fresh nutmeg.

Freeze in an ice cream maker according to the manufacturer's instructions. Transfer to a container, cover, and freeze until firm, about 2 hours.

MAKES ABOUT 1 QUART

Blueberry Ice Cream

It is wise to incorporate blueberries often in the diet, as they burst with healthful goodness from the natural antioxidant anthocyanin. Luckily, they're also delicious! This is a popular flavor at the Glacier Café in Glacier National Park in Montana. The ice cream also works beautifully with huckleberries.

2 cups (about 12 ounces) fresh blueberries

2 tablespoons water

2 teaspoons grated lemon zest

⅔ cup sugar, divided

1½ cups half-and-half or milk

1 cup heavy (whipping) cream

1 tablespoon freshly squeezed lemon juice

1 teaspoon vanilla extract

2 tablespoons honey liqueur or framboise (optional)

Rinse the berries and pick out any bad ones. Place in a small saucepan with the water and cook over low heat until tender, about 10 minutes. Let cool slightly and purée in a blender or food processor.

In a small bowl, mash the zest with 1 teaspoon of the sugar to release the oils. In a small saucepan, heat the half-and-half with the remaining sugar, stirring until dissolved; let cool to room temperature. Stir in the blueberry purée, cream, sugared zest, juice, and vanilla. Transfer to a container, cover, and refrigerate until thoroughly chilled, about 3 hours.

Freeze in an ice cream maker according to the manufacturer's instructions. When the ice cream is almost frozen, spoon in the liqueur, if desired, and churn until blended in, about 1 minute more. Transfer to a container, cover, and freeze until firm, about 2 hours.

MAKES ABOUT 1 QUART

Strega Semifreddo

Sugar syrup beaten into egg yolks creates an especially airy, mousselike ice cream called a *semifreddo*. In Italy, semifreddi are fashionable in both the gelateria and the upscale restaurants. Here it has a lovely flowery herb over-tone from the Italian liqueur Strega. If you can't find Strega, use sambuca for an anise scent or Grand Marnier for a brandied orange infusion.

⅔ cup sugar	2 teaspoons grated orange zest
¼ cup water	2 cups half-and-half
1 tablespoon light corn syrup	1 cup (heavy) whipping cream
4 large egg yolks	¼ cup Strega, sambuca, or Grand Marnier

Combine the sugar, water, and corn syrup in a small saucepan and bring to a boil. Cook until the temperature reaches 238°F on a candy thermometer (soft ball stage). Meanwhile, beat the egg yolks with an electric mixer until thick and pale yellow. Continuing to beat the egg yolks on medium speed, slowly pour in the sugar syrup in a fine, steady stream. Beat until the mixture cools to room temperature, about 7 minutes. Stir in the zest and half-and-half. Cover and refrigerate until thoroughly chilled, about 3 hours.

When ready to freeze, stir in the cream. Freeze in an ice cream maker according to the manufacturer's instructions. When the ice cream is almost frozen, spoon in the Strega and churn until blended in, about 1 minute more. Transfer to a container, cover, and freeze until firm, about 2 hours.

MAKES ABOUT 1 QUART

Lavender-Honey Ice Cream

French lavender is the best varietal to use for cooking, as it lends a delightful aromatic perfume with an intriguingly haunting overtone. Other lavender species have a more medicinal taste. Use either the fresh or dried blossoms, stripped from the stem. Honey liqueur is a perfect complement, and it creates a softer texture.

2 cups half-and-half or milk

3 tablespoons fresh or dried lavender blossoms

3 large egg yolks

⅔ cup honey

1 cup heavy (whipping) cream

2 to 3 tablespoons honey liqueur (optional)

Prepare a large bowl or pan of ice water.

In the top of a double boiler, heat the half-and-half and lavender over simmering water until steaming. Remove from the heat and steep for 10 minutes. In a bowl, whisk the egg yolks until blended, then whisk in the honey. Whisk in about half of the hot half-and-half and pour the yolk mixture into the pan of half-and-half. Stir and cook over simmering water until the custard coats the back of a silicone spatula or spoon, about 10 minutes. Immediately place the custard pan in the ice bath and stir the custard occasionally until it cools to room temperature. Strain the custard into a container and discard the lavender. Stir in the cream, cover, and refrigerate until thoroughly chilled, about 3 hours.

Freeze in an ice cream maker according to the manufacturer's instructions. When the ice cream is almost frozen, spoon in the honey liqueur, if desired, and churn until blended in, about 1 minute more. Transfer to a container, cover, and freeze until firm, about 2 hours.

MAKES ABOUT 1 QUART

Grand Marnier Ice Cream

Orange zest emphasizes the citrus overtones in this elegant ice cream. Pair it with individual warm chocolate cakes or a raspberry tart. Or serve scoopfuls with almond biscotti or lemon wafers.

2 teaspoons grated orange zest

⅔ cup sugar, divided

2 cups half-and-half or milk

4 large egg yolks

1 cup heavy (whipping) cream

3 tablespoons Grand Marnier or Cointreau

Prepare a large bowl or pan of ice water.

In a small bowl, mash the zest with 1 teaspoon of the sugar to release the oils. In the top of a double boiler, heat the half-and-half over simmering water until steaming. In a bowl, whisk the egg yolks until blended, then whisk in the remaining sugar and the sugared zest. Whisk in about half of the hot half-and-half and pour the yolk mixture into the pan of half-and-half. Stir and cook over simmering water until the custard coats the back of a silicone spatula or spoon, about 10 minutes. Immediately place the custard pan in the ice bath and stir the custard occasionally until it cools to room temperature. Transfer to a container and stir in the cream. Cover and refrigerate until thoroughly chilled, about 3 hours.

Freeze in an ice cream maker according to the manufacturer's instructions. When the ice cream is almost frozen, spoon in the Grand Marnier and churn until blended in, about 1 minute more. Transfer to a container, cover, and freeze until firm, about 2 hours.

MAKES ABOUT 1 QUART

Rum Raisin Ice Cream

I first discovered this winning combination—made with dark raisins—in Paris. Now I have switched to the sweeter golden ones. Plumped in rum, these tart-sweet nuggets polka-dot the ice cream. Let this top baked apples or poached pears. It is also delicious crowning slices of spice cake or a nut tart.

¾ cup golden raisins

¼ cup dark rum

2 cups half-and-half or milk

4 large egg yolks

⅔ cup sugar

1 cup heavy (whipping) cream

½ teaspoon vanilla extract

Prepare a large bowl or pan of ice water.

Place the raisins in a small microwavable bowl and pour on the rum; microwave on high 40 seconds or steep for 15 minutes.

In the top of a double boiler, heat the half-and-half over simmering water until steaming. In a bowl, whisk the egg yolks until blended, then whisk in the sugar. Whisk in about half of the hot half-and-half and pour the yolk mixture into the pan of half-and-half. Stir and cook over simmering water until the custard coats the back of a silicone spatula or spoon, about 10 minutes. Strain the raisins, reserving the rum, and stir them into the custard. Immediately place the custard pan in the ice bath and stir the custard occasionally until it cools to room temperature. Transfer to a container and stir in the cream and vanilla. Cover and refrigerate until thoroughly chilled, about 3 hours.

Freeze in an ice cream maker according to the manufacturer's instructions. When the ice cream is almost frozen, spoon in the reserved rum and churn until blended in, about 1 minute more. Transfer to a container, cover, and freeze until firm, about 2 hours.

MAKES ABOUT 1 QUART

GELATI &
FROZEN YOGURTS

THE SAMPLING OF DENSER ITALIAN-STYLE GELATI FEATURES

enticingly intense fruit flavors such as strawberry, mango, blood orange, and nectarine. The word gelato refers to various styles of ice cream, from light to richer versions. Delicious Strawberry and Ginger-Nectarine Frozen Yogurts provide a healthful snack and are great as a morning or afternoon refresher. Expect frozen yogurt to be denser than ice cream as it lacks the heavy cream that aerates ice cream. It is smart to let the container of frozen yogurt soften slightly in the refrigerator for 30 minutes before scooping.

Caramel-Cognac Gelato

A rich caramel flavor permeates this light-style Italian ice cream, which is laced with a shot of cognac. The added cornstarch helps to produce the denser texture of a classic gelato.

¾ cup sugar

½ cup water

2 tablespoons cornstarch

2 cups milk

¾ cup heavy (whipping) cream

1 teaspoon vanilla extract

2 tablespoons cognac, dark rum, or amaretto

Prepare a large bowl or pan of ice water.

Place the sugar in a medium saucepan and heat over medium heat, swirling the pan occasionally, until the sugar melts and caramelizes to a light amber color, 5 to 7 minutes. (Do not stir.) Be careful, as the sugar is very hot. (If the sugar should crystallize on the sides of the pan before melting, put a lid on the pan to help wash down the sugar crystals, rather than try to stir them in.) When the sugar is completely melted, carefully pour in the water—it will steam and bubble. Place the cornstarch in a bowl and stir ¼ cup of the milk into the cornstarch. Carefully add the remaining 1¾ cups milk to the caramel and continue to heat, stirring, until the caramel dissolves. Whisk in the cornstarch paste and cook over medium heat until the mixture thickens and comes to a boil. Immediately place the pan in the ice bath and stir the mixture occasionally until it cools to room temperature. Transfer to a container and stir in the cream and vanilla. Cover and refrigerate until thoroughly chilled, about 3 hours.

Freeze in an ice cream maker according to the manufacturer's instructions. When the ice cream is almost frozen, spoon in the cognac and churn until blended in, about 1 minute more. Transfer to a container, cover, and freeze until firm, about 2 hours.

MAKES ABOUT 1 QUART

White Chocolate–Framboise Truffle Gelato

Pair this white chocolate frosty gelato with chocolate soufflé cake for a winning party treat.

TRUFFLES

6 ounces bittersweet chocolate, chopped, or 1 cup chocolate chips

3 tablespoons heavy (whipping) cream

1 tablespoon unsalted butter

1 tablespoon framboise

1¾ cups half-and-half or milk

½ cup sugar

2 tablespoons cornstarch

⅛ teaspoon salt

8 ounces white chocolate, chopped

1¼ cups heavy (whipping) cream

1 teaspoon vanilla extract

2 tablespoons framboise (optional)

Prepare a large bowl or pan of ice water.

To make the Truffles: In the top of a double boiler, heat the chocolate, cream, and butter over simmering water, stirring until smooth. Stir in the framboise. Transfer to a small container and let cool. Cover and refrigerate until cold and firm, about 1 hour. Scoop out ½-teaspoon portions and drop them onto an aluminum foil–lined baking sheet. Cover and refrigerate until ready to use.

In a bowl, whisk together ½ cup of the half-and-half, the sugar, cornstarch, and salt. In a small saucepan, bring the remaining 1¼ cups half-and-half just to a boil over medium heat. Whisk in the sugar mixture and boil until thickened, about 2 to 3 minutes. Let cool to 110°F on a candy thermometer. Place the white chocolate in a heatproof bowl and pour the hot half-and-half over it. Stir until the chocolate is melted. Place the bowl in the ice bath and stir the mixture occasionally until it cools to room temperature. Stir in the cream and vanilla, cover, and refrigerate until thoroughly chilled, about 3 hours.

Freeze in an ice cream maker according to the manufacturer's instructions. When the ice cream is almost frozen, spoon in the framboise, if desired, and churn until blended in, about 1 minute more. Add the chocolate truffles and churn until blended in, about 15 seconds more. Transfer to a container, cover, and freeze until firm, about 2 hours.

MAKES ABOUT 1 QUART

Mango Gelato

This looks festive served in glass bowls with a pretty edible blossom, such as a nasturtium, violet, or calendula, tucked on top. Let it follow a salad luncheon or a Moroccan or Asian dinner menu featuring duck or grilled pork or chicken kebabs.

½ cup sugar

½ cup water

2 pounds ripe mangoes (about 2 large mangoes)

3 tablespoons freshly squeezed lime or lemon juice

⅔ cup heavy (whipping) cream

Prepare a large bowl or pan of ice water.

In a medium saucepan, combine the sugar and water, bring to a boil while stirring, and cook until the syrup is clear. Immediately place the pan in the ice bath and stir the mixture occasionally until it cools to room temperature.

Peel and dice the mangoes, discarding the seeds, and purée the mangoes in a blender or food processor with the juice and syrup. Transfer to a container and stir in the cream. Cover and refrigerate until thoroughly chilled, about 3 hours.

Freeze in an ice cream maker according to the manufacturer's instructions. Transfer to a container, cover, and freeze until firm, about 2 hours.

MAKES ABOUT 1 QUART

Nectarine-Ginger Frozen Yogurt

The spicy-hot accent of crystallized ginger teases extra flavor from sweet, ripe nectarines in this healthful dessert. Another time, pears would make a great stand-in for nectarines or peaches. If you can find Greek yogurt, it is an excellent choice for this dessert.

½ cup water

¼ cup sugar

One 1-inch piece fresh ginger, peeled and chopped

1 pound ripe nectarines or peaches (about 3 nectarines or peaches)

¼ cup honey

1 tablespoon freshly squeezed lemon juice

2 cups unflavored 2% or full-fat yogurt

⅓ cup diced crystallized ginger

Combine the water, sugar, and fresh ginger in a small saucepan and bring to a boil, stirring to dissolve the sugar. Cook until the syrup is clear. Remove from the heat and steep for 30 minutes. Strain the mixture into a large saucepan, discarding the ginger.

Halve and pit the nectarines (peel the peaches, if using), coarsely chop them, and add to the syrup with the honey and juice. Bring to a boil and cook on high heat, stirring occasionally, until the fruit is soft, about 10 minutes. Remove from the heat and let cool to room temperature. Transfer to a container and stir in the yogurt and crystallized ginger. Cover and refrigerate until thoroughly chilled, about 3 hours.

Freeze in an ice cream maker according to the manufacturer's instructions. Or, to freeze without an ice cream maker, pour the mixture into a 9-inch non-reactive square pan. Cover with aluminum foil or plastic wrap and freeze just until solid, 2 to 3 hours. Scrape out into an electric mixer or food processor and process briefly until light and fluffy. Serve at once or transfer to a container, cover, and freeze until firm, about 2 hours.

MAKES ABOUT 1 QUART

Blood Orange Gelato

Brilliant ruby orange juice exemplifies the sun-sweet tang of ripe citrus in this ultrarefreshing, light-style gelato. Cream gives it just a touch of richness. Partner this gelato with Tuscan biscotti or amaretti cookies.

1 tablespoon grated blood orange zest

⅔ cup sugar, divided

⅔ cup water

2 cups freshly squeezed blood orange juice

¼ cup freshly squeezed lemon juice

⅔ cup heavy (whipping) cream

Prepare a large bowl or pan of ice water.

In a small bowl, mash the zest with 1 teaspoon of the sugar to release the oils. Combine the remaining sugar and water in a medium saucepan and bring to a boil, stirring to dissolve the sugar. Cook until the syrup is clear. Remove from the heat and stir in the juices and sugared zest. Immediately place the pan in the ice bath and stir the mixture occasionally until it cools to room temperature. Transfer to a container and stir in the cream. Cover and refrigerate until thoroughly chilled, about 3 hours.

Freeze in an ice cream maker according to the manufacturer's instructions. Transfer to a container, cover, and freeze until firm, about 2 hours.

MAKES ABOUT 1 QUART

Strawberry Frozen Yogurt

This bright rosy-red yogurt carries an intense berry flavor that is mouth-wateringly aromatic. It is best served slightly soft, so let it thaw in the refrigerator for 30 minutes before serving.

2½ cups (about 1¼ pounds) fresh or frozen strawberries

½ cup sugar

¼ cup light corn syrup

2 tablespoons orange juice concentrate, thawed

1 tablespoon freshly squeezed lemon juice

2 cups unflavored 2% or full-fat yogurt

In a food processor or blender, purée the strawberries, sugar, corn syrup, orange juice concentrate, and juice. Let stand for 20 minutes for the sugar to dissolve. Blend in the yogurt. Cover and refrigerate until thoroughly chilled, about 3 hours.

Freeze in an ice cream maker according to the manufacturer's instructions. Or, to freeze without an ice cream maker, pour the mixture into a 9-inch nonreactive square pan. Cover with aluminum foil or plastic wrap and freeze just until solid, 2 to 3 hours. Scrape out into an electric mixer or food processor and process briefly until light and fluffy. Serve at once or transfer to a container, cover, and freeze until firm, about 2 hours.

MAKES ABOUT 1 QUART

SORBETS, ICES & GRANITE

A WEALTH OF FRUIT PURÉES AND JUICES ENHANCES THESE frosty confections for a refreshing sweet at all occasions. Some, like Rosemary-Lemon Ice, Green Apple Sorbet, and Shiraz Granita, are lovely as an intermezzo (between courses). Others, like Melon or Kiwi Fruit Sorbet, are fun to serve at brunch with a complementary fruit accompaniment. The Campari-Grapefuit Granita makes a delightful opener for brunch or dinner.

Green Apple Sorbet

I first sampled this lovely pale green sorbet in a Brussels café. It was prettily flecked with shavings of peel and was served in tall slender goblets, accented by apple mint sprigs. I utilized the Granny Smith apples hanging heavy in my garden to produce this unusual refresher. By coincidence, apple mint proliferates beneath this tree.

2 pounds Granny Smith apples (about 5 apples), cored and sliced (unpeeled)

3 tablespoons freshly squeezed lemon juice

1 cup water

¾ cup sugar

Fresh apple mint sprigs for garnish

Toss the apple slices with the juice, slip into a lock-top plastic bag, and freeze until firm, about 1 hour.

Combine the water and sugar in a small saucepan and bring to a boil, stirring to dissolve the sugar. Cook until the syrup is clear. Remove from the heat and let cool to room temperature. Transfer to a container, cover, and refrigerate until thoroughly chilled, about 3 hours.

In a food processor, blend the frozen apples and syrup just until light and fluffy. Serve at once in chilled goblets and garnish with mint sprigs. Or, transfer to a container, cover, and freeze until firm, about 2 hours.

MAKES ABOUT 1 ½ PINTS

Kiwi Fruit Sorbet

The snapping, crisp, black seeds of kiwi fruit lend a neat bite to this emerald green sorbet. Squeeze a lime wedge over each serving for added sparkle.

2 teaspoons grated lime or lemon zest

¾ cup sugar, divided

¾ cup water

2 pounds kiwi fruit (about 8 kiwi fruit), peeled and quartered

6 tablespoons freshly squeezed lime or lemon juice

2 limes, quartered

In a small bowl, mash the zest with 1 teaspoon of the sugar to release the oils. Combine the remaining sugar and water in a small saucepan and bring to a boil, stirring to dissolve the sugar. Cook until the syrup is clear. Remove from the heat and let cool to room temperature. In a food processor or blender, purée the kiwi fruit with the juice, syrup, and sugared zest. Transfer to a container, cover, and refrigerate until thoroughly chilled, about 3 hours.

Freeze in an ice cream maker according to the manufacturer's instructions. Or, to freeze without an ice cream maker, pour the mixture into a 9-inch nonreactive square pan. Cover with aluminum foil or plastic wrap and freeze just until solid, 2 to 3 hours. Scrape out into an electric mixer or food processor and process briefly until light and fluffy. Serve at once or transfer to a container, cover, and freeze until firm, about 2 hours. At serving time, garnish with a lime wedge to squeeze over each serving.

MAKES ABOUT 1 QUART

Variation:
Mango Sorbet: Substitute 2 pounds large mangoes (about 2 mangoes) for the kiwi fruit. When the sorbet is almost frozen, spoon in 2 tablespoons rum, and churn until blended in, about 1 minute more.

Melon Sorbet

The wide variety of melons available today offers many flavor potentials for sorbet. Pale green honeydew, rosy watermelon, or the golden Crenshaw, casaba, or cantaloupe are all ideal. Pick a melon at its peak of ripeness for best flavor. For a handsome presentation, surround the sorbet with melon balls in a contrasting color. Consider pairing a pale green melon with an orange-hued ice or a rosy pink melon with green-toned ice. Garnish with a pretty edible blossom.

About 3 pounds melon, peeled and seeded

¼ cup sugar

3 tablespoons freshly squeezed lime juice

Cut the melon into 1-inch cubes and purée it in a food processor (you should have about 3 cups). Combine the purée with the sugar and juice and stir until dissolved. Cover and refrigerate until thoroughly chilled, about 3 hours.

Pour into a 9-inch nonreactive square pan. Cover with aluminum foil or plastic wrap and freeze just until solid, 2 to 3 hours. Scrape out into a food processor or electric mixer and process briefly until light and fluffy. Serve at once or transfer to a container, cover, and freeze until firm, about 2 hours.

MAKES ABOUT 1 QUART

Raspberry-Citrus Sorbet

This is an elegant sorbet—a brilliant ruby color and bursting with flavor. (A strawberry version is almost as good.) In the Italian tradition, I love to mingle tiny scoopfuls with ice cream flavors—Hazelnut Ice Cream (page 29) and Peach Ice Cream (page 43) are divine with it. Or serve it with a medley of fresh strawberries and raspberries.

4 cups (about 2 pounds) fresh or
  frozen raspberries

1 cup freshly squeezed orange juice

⅓ cup freshly squeezed lemon juice

¾ cup sugar

3 tablespoons Cointreau or other
  orange-flavored liqueur

Purée the berries in a food processor or blender and push them through a fine-mesh sieve into a bowl; discard the seeds. Stir in the juices and sugar until dissolved. Cover and refrigerate until thoroughly chilled, about 3 hours.

Freeze in an ice cream maker according to the manufacturer's instructions. When the sorbet is almost frozen, spoon in the liqueur, and churn until blended in, about 1 minute more. Or, to freeze without an ice cream maker, pour the mixture into a 9-inch nonreactive square pan. Cover with aluminum foil or plastic wrap and freeze just until solid, 2 to 3 hours. Scrape out into an electric mixer or food processor, spoon in the liqueur, and process briefly until light and fluffy. Serve at once or transfer to a container, cover, and freeze until firm, about 2 hours.

MAKES ABOUT 1 QUART

Dark Chocolate Sorbet

A spoonful of a favorite liquor or liqueur lends a heady uplift to this rich, deep, dark brown sorbet and it also softens the texture to a lovely spoonable consistency. It is important to swirl the pan, rather than stir the sugar as it caramelizes, to avoid crystallization.

1 cup sugar

3 cups water, divided

¾ cup unsweetened cocoa powder

¼ teaspoon salt

3 tablespoons dark rum, Grand Marnier, cognac, or amaretto

Prepare a large bowl or pan of ice water.

Combine the sugar and 2 tablespoons of the water in a medium saucepan and heat over medium heat, swirling the pan occasionally, until the sugar melts and caramelizes to a light amber color, 5 to 7 minutes. (Do not stir.) Be careful, as the sugar is very hot. (If the sugar should crystallize on the sides of the pan before melting, put a lid on the pan to help wash down the sugar crystals, rather than try to stir them in.) When the sugar is completely melted, carefully pour in the remaining water and continue to heat, stirring, until the caramel dissolves. Whisk in the cocoa and salt. Immediately place the pan in the ice bath and stir the mixture occasionally until it cools to room temperature. Transfer to a container, cover, and refrigerate until thoroughly chilled, about 3 hours.

Freeze in an ice cream maker according to the manufacturer's instructions. When the mixture is almost frozen, spoon in the alcohol, and churn until blended in, about 1 minute more. Or, to freeze without an ice cream maker, pour the mixture into a 9-inch nonreactive square pan. Cover with aluminum foil or plastic wrap and freeze just until solid, 2 to 3 hours. Scrape out into an electric mixer or food processor, spoon in the alcohol, and process briefly until light and fluffy. Serve at once or transfer to a container, cover, and freeze until firm, about 2 hours.

MAKES ABOUT 1 QUART

Rosemary-Lemon Ice

This herbal-scented ice wakes up the palate when served as an intermezzo (between courses). Or, cut back on the rosemary if you wish to pair it with another fruit sorbet for a summertime dessert.

1 tablespoon grated lemon zest

¾ cup sugar, divided

2 cups water

Four 4-inch sprigs rosemary plus extra for garnish

¾ cup freshly squeezed lemon juice

In a small bowl, mash the zest with 1 teaspoon of the sugar to release the oils. Combine the remaining sugar, water, and 4 rosemary sprigs in a medium saucepan and bring to a boil, stirring to dissolve the sugar. Cook until the syrup is clear. Remove from the heat and stir in the sugared zest and juice. Let cool to room temperature. Transfer to a container, cover, and refrigerate until thoroughly chilled, about 3 hours.

Remove the rosemary sprigs. Freeze in an ice cream maker according to the manufacturer's instructions. Or, to freeze without an ice cream maker, pour the mixture into a 9-inch nonreactive square pan. Cover with aluminum foil or plastic wrap and freeze just until solid, 2 to 3 hours. Scrape out into an electric mixer or food processor and process briefly until light and fluffy. Serve at once or transfer to a container, cover, and freeze until firm, about 2 hours. Serve in small bowls or goblets with a small garnish of rosemary.

MAKES ABOUT 1 QUART

Pear-Riesling Sorbet

Choose flavorful ripe pears such as Anjou, Comice, or Bosc for this delicate sorbet. It is delightful concluding a dinner featuring roast chicken, duck, or soy-glazed pork tenderloin.

2½ pounds large pears (about 5 pears), peeled, cored, and sliced

1 cup water

1 cup semisweet white wine, such as Riesling, Semillon, or Chenin Blanc

¾ cup sugar

1 tablespoon freshly squeezed lemon juice

¼ teaspoon freshly grated nutmeg

½ cup heavy (whipping) cream

2 to 3 tablespoons pear brandy (optional)

Combine the pears, water, wine, sugar, juice, and nutmeg in a medium saucepan. Bring to a boil, reduce heat, and simmer until the pears are soft and the alcohol has evaporated, about 10 minutes. Let cool to room temperature. Transfer to a container and stir in the cream. Cover and refrigerate until thoroughly chilled, about 3 hours.

Freeze in an ice cream maker according to the manufacturer's instructions. When the sorbet is almost frozen, spoon in the brandy, if desired, and churn until blended in, about 1 minute more. Or, to freeze without an ice cream maker, pour the mixture into a 9-inch nonreactive square pan. Cover with aluminum foil or plastic wrap and freeze just until solid, 2 to 3 hours. Scrape out into an electric mixer or food processor, spoon in the brandy, if using, and process briefly until light and fluffy. Serve at once or transfer to a container, cover, and freeze until firm, about 2 hours.

MAKES ABOUT 1 QUART

Lime Ice

Pale green and wonderfully zingy, this citrus ice gets raves. Serve it with a sprig of mint or lemon balm or pair it with sliced mango or papaya. It's especially good served after a Mexican or Caribbean dinner. You might even use it to make a stellar frozen margarita.

2 tablespoons grated lime zest	2 cups water
¾ cup sugar, divided	1 cup freshly squeezed lime juice

In a small bowl, mash the zest with 1 teaspoon of the sugar to release the oils. Combine the remaining sugar and the water in a medium saucepan and bring to a boil, stirring to dissolve the sugar. Cook until the syrup is clear. Remove from the heat and stir in the sugared zest and juice. Let cool to room temperature. Transfer to a container, cover, and refrigerate until thoroughly chilled, about 3 hours.

Freeze in an ice cream maker according to the manufacturer's instructions. Or, to freeze without an ice cream maker, pour the mixture into a 9-inch nonreactive square pan. Cover with aluminum foil or plastic wrap and freeze just until solid, 2 to 3 hours. Scrape out into an electric mixer or food processor and process briefly until light and fluffy. Serve at once or transfer to a container, cover, and freeze until firm, about 2 hours.

MAKES ABOUT 1 QUART

Variations:

Lemon Ice: Use lemon zest in place of lime zest. Increase the sugar by 2 tablespoons and reduce the water to 1¾ cups. Use only ¾ cup freshly squeezed lemon juice in place of the lime juice. After scraping the frozen mixture from the pan, spoon 2 tablespoons dry white wine or champagne into the mixer and process as directed.

Meyer Lemon Ice: Use lemon zest in place of lime zest. Reduce the sugar to ⅔ cup and use ¾ cup freshly squeezed Meyer lemon juice plus 3 tablespoons regular lemon juice in place of the lime juice.

Three Citrus Ice

This zesty ice is a combination of three flavorful citrus juices. If you have blood oranges, tangerines, or Meyer lemons, try any of those in the mixture. The ice looks festive served with a sprig of lemon balm or an edible blossom such as an unsprayed violet or pansy from the garden.

2 teaspoons grated lemon zest

½ cup sugar, divided

½ cup water

1½ cups freshly squeezed orange juice

1¼ cups freshly squeezed grapefruit juice

¼ cup freshly squeezed lemon juice

In a small bowl, mash the zest with 1 teaspoon of the sugar to release the oils. Combine the remaining sugar and water in a medium saucepan and bring to a boil, stirring to dissolve the sugar. Cook until the syrup is clear. Remove from the heat and stir in the juices and sugared zest. Let cool to room temperature. Transfer to a container, cover, and refrigerate until thoroughly chilled, about 3 hours.

Freeze in an ice cream maker according to the manufacturer's instructions. Or, to freeze without an ice cream maker, pour the mixture into a 9-inch non-reactive square pan. Cover with aluminum foil or plastic wrap and freeze just until solid, 2 to 3 hours. Scrape out into an electric mixer or food processor and process briefly until light and fluffy. Serve at once or transfer to a container, cover, and freeze until firm, about 2 hours.

MAKES ABOUT 1 QUART

Espresso Granita

In Italy, under the canopies on the piazza, tourists and natives slurp this as a popular refresher on a summer day. Top it with brandy and whipped cream for an authentic touch.

½ cup sugar

½ cup water

3 tablespoons unsweetened cocoa powder

3 cups espresso or triple-strength coffee

½ teaspoon vanilla extract

Brandy for garnish

Whipped cream for garnish (optional)

Combine the sugar, water, and cocoa in a medium saucepan and bring to a boil, stirring to dissolve the sugar. Cook until the syrup is clear. Remove from the heat and stir in the espresso and vanilla. Let cool to room temperature. Transfer to a container, cover, and refrigerate until thoroughly chilled, about 3 hours.

Pour into a 9-inch nonreactive square pan, cover with aluminum foil or plastic wrap, and place in the freezer. Once an hour, stir with a fork, scraping the crystals from the sides of the pan into the liquid center. Repeat 2 or 3 times until the entire mass is set into small, light crystals, 2 to 3 hours. Serve at once or transfer to a container, cover, and freeze. To serve, spoon into chilled parfait or other decorative glasses, letting it mound on the surface, and pour 1 teaspoon of brandy over each serving. Top with whipped cream, if desired.

MAKES ABOUT 1 QUART

Shiraz Granita

The full-flavored Shiraz (or Syrah) wine imparts berrylike fruitiness to this icy refresher. Other dry red wines would work very well, too. Serve between courses, if you wish, or as a summertime dessert with biscotti. When Bing cherries are in season, they are lovely dressing it up as a garnish. Another time, adorn it with edible flowers such as unsprayed violets from the garden.

½ cup sugar

½ cup water

2 cups dry red wine, such as Shiraz, Merlot, or Zinfandel

⅓ cup freshly squeezed orange juice

3 tablespoons freshly squeezed lemon juice

1 cup pitted Bing cherries for garnish

Edible flowers, mint, or lemon balm sprigs for garnish (optional)

Combine the sugar and water in a medium saucepan and bring to a boil, stirring to dissolve the sugar. Cook until the syrup is clear. Remove from the heat and stir in the wine and juices. Let cool to room temperature. Transfer to a container, cover, and refrigerate until thoroughly chilled, about 3 hours.

Pour into a 9-inch nonreactive square pan, cover with aluminum foil or plastic wrap, and place in the freezer. Every 2 hours, stir with a fork, scraping the crystals from the sides of the pan into the liquid center. Repeat 5 or 6 times until the entire mass is set into small, light crystals, up to 12 hours. Serve at once or transfer to a container, cover, and freeze. To serve, spoon into chilled wine or other decorative glasses, letting it mound on the surface. Garnish with cherries and flowers, mint, or lemon balm, if desired.

MAKES ABOUT 1½ PINTS

Watermelon Granita

Both lime and orange zests intensify the melon fruitiness in this rosy-pink granita. For a striking presentation, serve a scoopful on a bed of sliced strawberries and green grapes.

2 teaspoons grated lime zest

2 teaspoons grated orange zest

⅔ cup sugar, divided

½ cup water

½ cup freshly squeezed orange juice

¼ cup freshly squeezed lime juice

2 pounds seedless watermelon, peeled

Fresh mint sprigs for garnish

In a small bowl, mash the zests with 1 teaspoon of the sugar to release the oils. Combine the remaining sugar, the water, and juices in a medium saucepan and bring to a boil, stirring to dissolve the sugar. Cook until the syrup is clear. Remove from the heat and stir in the sugared zests. Let cool to room temperature.

Cut the watermelon into 1-inch cubes and purée it in a food processor (you should have about 2⅓ cups). Stir in the sugar syrup, cover, and refrigerate until thoroughly chilled, about 3 hours.

Pour into a 9-inch nonreactive square pan, cover with aluminum foil or plastic wrap, and place in the freezer. Once an hour, stir with a fork, scraping the crystals from the sides of the pan into the liquid center. Repeat 2 or 3 times until the entire mass is set into small, light crystals, 2 to 3 hours. Serve at once or transfer to a container, cover, and freeze. To serve, spoon into dessert bowls and garnish with mint.

MAKES ABOUT 1 QUART

Lemongrass-Wine Ice

The stalks of lemongrass have an outer sheath that must be peeled off to reveal the fragrant core. Lemongrass and ginger make a lively duo with heat, spice, and an exotic overtone. This is ideal to conclude spicy fare, such as an Indian or Thai menu. If you can't find fresh lemongrass, check your grocery produce section for puréed lemongrass in a tube.

Four 6-inch stalks lemongrass	¾ cup sugar
2½ cups dry white wine	¾ cup water
One 1-inch piece fresh ginger, peeled and chopped	2 tablespoons freshly squeezed lemon juice

Peel the lemongrass and chop it into ¼-inch chunks. Combine the lemongrass, wine, and ginger in a medium saucepan and bring to a boil. Remove from the heat and steep for 30 minutes.

Combine the sugar and water in a medium saucepan and bring to a boil, stirring to dissolve the sugar. Cook until the syrup is clear. Remove from the heat and let cool to room temperature. Strain the wine mixture into a container, discarding the lemongrass and ginger, and stir into the sugar syrup along with the juice. Let cool further if needed. Cover, and refrigerate until thoroughly chilled, about 3 hours.

Freeze in an ice cream maker according to the manufacturer's instructions. Or, to freeze without an ice cream maker, pour the mixture into a 9-inch non-reactive square pan. Cover with aluminum foil or plastic wrap and freeze just until solid, 2 to 3 hours. Scrape out into an electric mixer or food processor and process briefly until light and fluffy. Serve at once or transfer to a container, cover, and freeze until firm, about 2 hours.

MAKES ABOUT 1 QUART

Campari-Grapefruit Granita

Serve this tangy refresher in wine goblets at a weekend brunch. It makes a neat stand-in for a beverage.

½ cup sugar

½ cup water

2½ cups freshly squeezed pink grapefruit juice (from 3 large pink grapefruit) with some pulp

¼ cup Campari

Grated grapefruit zest, fresh mint, or lemon balm for garnish

Combine the sugar and water in a medium saucepan and bring to a boil, stirring to dissolve the sugar. Cook until the syrup is clear. Remove from the heat and stir in the juice and Campari. Let cool to room temperature. Transfer to a container, cover, and refrigerate until thoroughly chilled, about 3 hours.

Pour into a 9-inch nonreactive square pan, cover with aluminum foil or plastic wrap, and place in the freezer. Once an hour, stir with a fork, scraping the crystals from the sides of the pan into the liquid center. Repeat 2 or 3 times until the entire mass is set into small, light crystals, 2 to 3 hours. Serve at once or transfer to a container, cover, and freeze. To serve, spoon into chilled wine glasses, letting it mound on the surface. Garnish with zest, mint, or lemon balm.

MAKES ABOUT 1 QUART

TOPPINGS & SAUCES

THE FILLIP AND SPECIAL FLOURISH TO A DISH OF ICE CREAM or sorbet can vary from a rich hot fudge sauce or butterscotch caramel sauce to an inviting multiberry compote or blackberry syrup. And for a finale sprinkled over all, caramelized nuts and praline lend a candy-like crunch to a frosty bowlful of gelato. Don't feel limited to these toppings, though! There are many garnishes available to complement every flavor of frozen dessert—from simple puréed fresh fruit to gourmet packaged sauces.

Maple-Pecan Sauce

This versatile sauce is a great addition to such ice cream flavors as Kona Coffee (page 28), Peach (page 43), and Classic Vanilla Bean (page 17).

4 tablespoons (½ stick) unsalted butter

⅓ cup confectioners' sugar

¼ cup pure maple syrup

¼ cup water

½ cup (2 ounces) toasted chopped pecans

1 tablespoon cognac

Melt the butter in a small saucepan over medium heat and cook until it just starts to turn brown. Let cool slightly and gradually stir in the sugar. Stir in the syrup and water and heat to boiling. Boil for 1 minute, stirring constantly. Stir in the nuts and cognac. Serve warm or cover and refrigerate for up to two weeks. Reheat in the top of a double boiler or in a microwave on high heat for 45 seconds.

MAKES ABOUT 1 CUP

Vanilla Bean Whipped Cream

The fruit pods of the vanilla plant yield the chocolate-brown slender beans, which when slit yield a multitude of black specks—the prized vanilla flavoring. If you bury a slit bean in confectioners' sugar it will release its perfume, ready to enhance many dishes.

One 3-inch piece vanilla bean

2 tablespoons confectioners' sugar

¾ cup heavy (whipping) cream

Slit the vanilla bean with a sharp paring knife and scrape the seeds into the sugar. Let stand for an hour or longer, if possible. In a small deep bowl, whip the cream until soft peaks form, then beat in the sugar. Cover and refrigerate for up to 1 day. Serve as a gala finish over berries or peaches topping ice cream.

MAKES ABOUT 1½ CUPS

Mocha Sauce

The aroma of coffee uplifts this warm chocolate sauce for a neat companion to Blueberry (page 45), Kona Coffee (page 28), or Classic Vanilla Bean (page 17) ice creams.

½ cup unsweetened cocoa powder

½ cup sugar

1 tablespoon instant espresso or coffee powder

½ cup half-and-half

2 tablespoons unsalted butter

1 teaspoon vanilla extract

Stir together the cocoa, sugar, and espresso powder in a medium saucepan. Stir in the half-and-half and cook over medium heat until the mixture comes to a boil. Reduce heat and let simmer for 2 minutes. Remove from the heat and stir in the butter and vanilla. Serve warm or at room temperature. Or, cover and refrigerate for up to 2 weeks. Reheat in a pan of hot water or in a heatproof container in a microwave on high heat for 30 seconds.

MAKES ABOUT 1 CUP

Butterscotch Caramel Sauce

Serve this brown sugar sauce warm so it flows over the ice cream. It's terrific topping Toasted Almond Ice Cream (page 29).

¾ cup packed dark brown sugar

⅓ cup light corn syrup

2 tablespoons unsalted butter

1 tablespoon water

Dash of salt

3 tablespoons heavy (whipping) cream

½ teaspoon vanilla extract

Combine the sugar, corn syrup, butter, water, and salt in a small saucepan. Bring to a boil over medium heat and boil 1 minute, or until the mixture has the consistency of heavy cream. Remove from the heat and let cool for 15 minutes, then stir in the cream and vanilla. Serve warm or cover and refrigerate for up to 2 weeks. Reheat in the top of a double boiler or in a microwave on high heat for 45 seconds.

MAKES ABOUT ¾ CUP

Framboise Sauce

This brilliant ruby berry sauce adds a burst of fresh flavor to desserts like Peach Ice Cream (page 43), and Lemon Ice (page 75).

2½ cups (about 1¼ pounds) fresh raspberries

¼ cup sugar

2 tablespoons freshly squeezed lemon juice

1 to 2 tablespoons framboise or other raspberry liqueur

Purée the berries in a food processor or blender and press through a fine-mesh sieve into a bowl; discard the seeds. Stir in the sugar, juice, and 1 tablespoon of the framboise. Taste and add more framboise as desired. Serve immediately or cover and refrigerate for up to 3 hours.

MAKES ABOUT 1½ CUPS

Summer Berry Compote

A mélange of berries picked at peak season makes a sumptuous topping on ice cream—not only on Classic Vanilla Bean Ice Cream (page 17), but also just as lovely on Grand Marnier (page 50) or Mango Gelato (page 56).

1½ cups (about 12 ounces) fresh
 strawberries, hulled and sliced

1 cup (about 8 ounces) fresh raspberries

1 cup (about 8 ounces) fresh
 blackberries or blueberries

2 tablespoons sugar

1 tablespoon honey liqueur or
 Cointreau (optional)

In a large bowl, toss together the berries and sugar. Let stand until the sugar dissolves. Stir in the liqueur, if desired. Serve at room temperature or cover and refrigerate for up to 3 hours.

MAKES ABOUT 3 CUPS

Note: If desired, replace the liqueur with 1 tablespoon 10-year-old or well-aged balsamic vinegar for a piquant flavor.

Blackberry-Balsamic Syrup

Well-aged balsamic vinegar has a smooth, mellow sweetness to it. Here it intensifies the fruity tang of blackberries in this deep violet syrup.

3 cups (about 1½ pounds) blackberries

⅔ cup sugar

½ cup water

1 tablespoon 5- or 10-year-old
balsamic vinegar

Combine the berries, sugar, water, and vinegar in a medium saucepan and bring to a boil. Reduce heat and simmer uncovered, stirring occasionally, until the fruit is soft, about 10 minutes. Let cool to room temperature. Purée in a food processor or blender and press through a fine-mesh sieve into a bowl; discard the seeds. Serve at room temperature or cover and refrigerate for up to 5 days.

MAKES ABOUT 1½ CUPS

Sticky Hot Fudge Sauce

This luscious chocolate sauce is reminiscent of the fudge sundaes served decades ago at Blum's, a renowned San Francisco pastry and ice cream shop.

6 ounces bittersweet or semisweet
chocolate, chopped, or 1 cup
chocolate chips

½ cup half-and-half

¼ cup light corn syrup

1 teaspoon vanilla extract

1 tablespoon Grand Marnier, brandy,
or cognac (optional)

Combine the chocolate, half-and-half, and corn syrup in the top of a double boiler, and heat over simmering water, stirring until smooth. Stir in the vanilla and Grand Marnier, if desired. Serve warm or at room temperature or cover and refrigerate for up to 2 weeks. Reheat in a pan of hot water or in a heatproof container in a microwave on high heat for 30 seconds.

MAKES ABOUT 1⅓ CUPS

Candied Cardamom Pecans

Spicy caramel-cloaked pecans make a handy topping on a wide variety of both ice cream and sorbet flavors.

1 tablespoon honey

1 tablespoon packed dark brown sugar

1 tablespoon water

½ teaspoon ground cardamom or ground cinnamon

1 cup (4 ounces) pecans

1 teaspoon unsalted butter, melted, plus extra for greasing

½ teaspoon vanilla extract

Preheat the oven to 350°F. Line a baking sheet with sides with aluminum foil and grease it lightly. In a small, heavy saucepan, heat the honey, sugar, water, and cardamom over medium heat until it comes a boil, then simmer 2 minutes. Mix in the nuts and stir to coat thoroughly, about 1 minute. Turn out onto the foil-lined pan. Bake until lightly toasted, about 8 to 10 minutes. Remove from the foil and place in a bowl. Combine the butter and vanilla and toss with the hot nuts. Store in an airtight container for up to 2 weeks.

MAKES 1 CUP

INDEX

TABLE OF EQUIVALENTS

The exact equivalents in the following tables have been rounded for convenience.

LIQUID/DRY MEASURES

U.S.	METRIC
¼ teaspoon	1.25 milliliters
½ teaspoon	2.5 milliliters
1 teaspoon	5 milliliters
1 tablespoon (3 teaspoons)	15 milliliters
1 fluid ounce (2 tablespoons)	30 milliliters
¼ cup	60 milliliters
⅓ cup	80 milliliters
½ cup	120 milliliters
1 cup	240 milliliters
1 pint (2 cups)	480 milliliters
1 quart (4 cups, 32 ounces)	960 milliliters
1 gallon (4 quarts)	3.84 liters
1 ounce (by weight)	28 grams
1 pound	454 grams
2.2 pounds	1 kilogram

OVEN TEMPERATURE

FAHRENHEIT	CELSIUS	GAS
250	120	½
275	140	1
300	150	2
325	160	3
350	180	4
375	190	5
400	200	6
425	220	7
450	230	8
475	240	9
500	260	10

LENGTH

U.S.	METRIC
⅛ inch	3 millimeters
¼ inch	6 millimeters
½ inch	12 millimeters
1 inch	2.5 centimeters